"10 Steps to Your First Sm.
by Strategy Scout, LLC

Printed in the United States of America

Third Edition

MyFirstSmallBusiness.com
contact@myfirstsmallbusiness.com

Any content posted, disseminated or made available in this book shall not, in any way, be construed as a guarantee of any certain result, or any specific future earnings. Any such content is provided for information purposes only, and should not be relied upon as the basis for any legal, financial, medical, tax or related decision.

Start Here

Welcome to the *10 Steps to Your First Small Business*! It is designed to be a simple and easy way to start your very own business.

We've tried to make this book very simple. Just start with Step 1 and follow the directions. Don't move to the next step until you have completed the previous steps. Once you have completed all 10 steps you will have your very own business!

In just a few moments we will start with the first step. Before we start here are the answers to four big questions that you may be wondering:

What if I don't have a business idea?
It is 'okay' if you do not have a business idea. This book will help you come up with some ideas. However, if you already have an idea that's great - this guide will show you how to tell if it is a good idea.

What if I don't have any money to start a business?
Having money to start a business is certainly helpful, however, there are plenty of businesses that you can start without money.

Also, if you start a business without money and the business does not do so well the only thing you have lost is your time. However, if you spend money to start a business and it does not do so well you have lost your time and money.

So, it is for this reason that you are encouraged to start your business with no money or as little money as possible.

How long will each of the 10 steps take?
The answer is that it is up to you.

Here's the thing: If you are serious about starting a business you want to ensure that you are taking your time doing it right from the start.

However, at the same time you don't want it to drag on. The longer you take to get through this plan the longer it will be before you can start your business - and start making money.

Will I make money quickly?
This is not a 'get rich quick' plan. You are not even guaranteed to make any money. Building a business - and making real money - takes hard work and determination. This book is meant for someone who is willing to put in the hard work and has the determination.

Ok, now that we have that covered let's get started by understanding exactly what you are getting into. We are going to do that by looking at how a business works. Let's go!

How a Business Works

Before we dive right into building your business we first need to step back and understand what a business is and how it works. People try to make 'business' difficult but it is really an easy concept.

A business simply sells something that someone else wants.

That's it.

All a business does is sell something (the product or service) to someone else (the customer) that they would want.

Think about it. McDonald's has been in business since 1955. They have been in business for that long because they sell something that someone else wants.

Nike has been in business since 1964. They have been in business for that long because they sell something that someone else wants.

People try to make business complicated. It is not that hard - you just simply must sell something that someone else wants.

One More Thing

It is true that all a business does is provide something that someone wants. If you don't have something that someone else wants then you are out of business - plain and simple.

But, you must do one more thing - you must provide something someone wants and make a profit.

Profit is what you get to keep. This is the money that goes in your wallet. This is the money that you get to spend on yourself.

Profit is simply:

$$Income - Expenses = Profit$$

Income is the money coming in to your business. The customer gives you money in exchange for what you are providing to them.

Expenses is the money going out of your business for things that help you run your business.

Here's an example:

Let's say it cost McDonald's $3 to make a Big Mac (this includes the bun, the meat, cheese, lettuce, special sauce, etc...) and they sell it to the customer for $5.

If a customer walks into McDonald's and buys one Big Mac then McDonald's profit would look like this...

$$Income - Expenses = Profit$$
$$\$5 - \$3 = \$2$$

McDonald's made a profit of $2.

(Now, McDonald's still has to pay other expenses like it's employees, the light bill, water bill, etc. But for the sake of simplicity we'll exclude that for now).

It would be crazy for McDonald's to charge $1 for a Big Mac if it cost them $3 to make. They would lose money!

So, it's not enough to sell something that someone else wants - you must also make a profit while doing so.

Now we get to the fun part. In Step 1 you are going to start coming up with ideas for what you want your business to do.

When you are ready to get started go to Step 1 on the next page.

Step 1: What Do You Want Your Business to Do?

In this step you are going to come up with a business idea.

Remember, you need to come up with a business idea that *sells something that someone else will want and will make a profit.*

Let's start coming up with ideas on what your future customers will want.

Now, it's not enough to simply come up with just *any* idea. You see, you are unique. You have unique skills, talents, interests, and abilities.

There is no one else on earth like you. So, you want to come up with a business idea that is unique to you.

You don't want to be just like everyone else. To help come up with a good business idea that is unique to you just answer these three questions.

#1. What kinds of things **interest** you?
#2. What kinds of things **are you good at**?
#3. What kinds of things **are people willing to pay for**?

Now, your business idea must meet all three of these things. Not one, not two - but all three things.

Why is that?

Let's say that Billy enjoys basketball. That is an interest of his. This meets question #1.

And, people are willing to pay for someone to be a basketball player. That is why the NBA exists. This meets question #3.

However, if Billy is short and has zero basketball skills then he does not meet the #2 question.

Here's another example. Let's say that there is a huge need in Steve's town for people to dig big holes (for planting trees). That meets question #3. People would be willing to pay Steve to dig big holes in the ground.

And, guess what, Steve is pretty good at digging holes. He has a shovel. He has arms. Steve meets question #2.

But, he does not have any interest - at all - in digging holes. Well then, this is not a business for Steve. He does not meet question #1.

One more example. Let's say that Sally has an interest in reading Harry Potter books. And, Sally is a pretty good reader.

She meets questions #1 and #2.

But (you probably saw this coming) do you think anyone will pay Sally to read Harry Potter books? No - and therefore she does not meet question #3.

The reason why you need to meet all three question requirements is because when you experience failure or setbacks in your business it is much easier to keep going if you are doing something that interests you and are good at.

And, of course, to stay in business it must be something that people are willing to pay you for.

The Importance of a Solid Business Idea

In just a few moments you are going to start brainstorming ideas on what you can provide to customers based on the three requirements:

#1. It must interest you.
#2. You must be good at it.
#3. Someone must be willing to pay you for it.

Before you start you should know that coming up with your business idea is a very important step. The rest of the 9 steps will not go well if you do not start off with a solid idea.

Because it is such an important step it may take you a few days to come up with a good idea. That is okay. It is better to not rush through this step.

One more thing, we'll worry about making sure you will make a profit later. For now, let's just come up with your business idea based on the three requirements.

Business Plan Notebook

In just a few moments you will write down as many ideas as you can come up with. If you haven't already, get a notebook that you can take notes in. This will be your Business Plan Notebook.

Ok, in your notebook write down as many business ideas that you can come up with (that meet all 3 of the requirements). Below is a list of 50 business ideas that can help you brainstorm some ideas.

50 Business Ideas

Use the list below to help you brainstorm some business ideas of your own.

- Lawn care and grass cutting service
- Sewing and knitting service
- Selling homemade crafts online (e.g. Etsy)
- Selling crafts at shows/fairs
- Pet sitting
- Dog walking service
- Pet cleaning/bathing service
- Babysitting
- Weekend nanny service
- Snow shoveling
- Leaf/pine straw raking
- Selling pine straw for landscaping
- Pool cleaning

- Pastry/cake/cupcake maker
- Cake decoration
- House cleaning service
- Pressure washing service
- Tutoring kids
- Music lessons for kids
- Delivering newspapers
- Making homemade jewelry
- Computer repair
- Computer help for seniors
- Electronic installation service
- Gift wrapping service
- Holiday decorating service
- Social media marketing services for businesses
- Website design
- Selling products on your own website
- Selling products on Amazon
- Virtual assisting
- Create and sell gift baskets
- Selling vintage/old items on eBay
- Selling other people's items on eBay or Craigslist
- Birthday party planner
- Photographer for birthday parties & other events
- Garden care/maintenance

- House painting service
- Video game swap/sell
- Sell food/drink items at fairs, shows, and sidewalk sales
- Grocery purchase & delivery service
- Graphic design
- Car detailing/wash service
- Moving service
- Writing or blogging service for businesses
- Magic/Puppet show performer
- Light housework/repair for the elderly
- Window washing service
- Grow and sell fruits & vegetables
- Video/photo editing service

Your Top Three

You just came up with a list of business ideas that meet the three requirements:

#1. It must interest you.
#2. You must be good at it.
#3. Someone must be willing to pay you for it.

In just a few moments you are going to narrow all your ideas down to find your top three ideas and then, ultimately, your top idea - which will become your business.

Ok, now, go through your list of business ideas that you wrote down in your notebook and think about which ideas you think people will want the most. Think about which ideas interest you the most. And, think about which ideas you think you will be particularly good at.

Based on everything that you have thought about circle your top three ideas in your notebook.

Trusted Advisor

Now that you have determined top three ideas you should get the opinion of an adult that you trust.

You can ask your parents, grandparents, older siblings, your teacher, your coach - really any adult that you trust.

You can ask your friends, but here's the thing, they are going to tell you what you want to hear. You need someone who can tell you the truth and be honest with you. If you feel like your friends can do that then ask them. But, still ask some trusted adults as well.

Ok, now, show someone you trust your top three business ideas and ask them for their feedback.

Your Top Idea

Now that you have gotten the opinion from a trusted adult you are about to narrow your top three ideas down to find your top business idea.

Remember, a business needs two things:

#1. It needs to provide something that someone else wants
#2. And, it needs to be able to make a profit

In just a few moments you are going to decide which of your three ideas will become your business. To help you decided here are six 'yes or no' questions.

Go through the questions and answer them with a 'yes' or 'no' while thinking about each of your top three business ideas.

Hopefully, after answering the questions it will become apparent what your top business idea is.

Question #1: Does the business solve a real need or problem that a lot of people are facing?

Question #2: Will your product or service be something that people want?

Question #3: Will you easily be able to find the type of people who would be willing to buy what your business is selling?

Question #4: Is this something that you think people will be willing to pay money for?

Question #5: Is this something that you can run yourself after school, on the weekends and in the summer?

Question #6: Can you start this business with equipment or supplies that you already own, or can borrow, or purchase very inexpensively?

Ok, now, based on the answers to those six questions write your top business idea in your notebook.

Congrats! You have your business idea. The fun is really about to begin.

You have completed Step 1. When you are ready go to Step 2.

Step 2: What Will Your Business Sell?

In Step 1 you have determined what you want your business to do. In this step you are going to clarify exactly what you are going to sell.

Think of a menu board when you walk into a fast-food restaurant. Everything the restaurant sells is in one place. This is what you will do in this step. You are going to list everything that you will sell to your customers.

Don't worry about prices right now. We will do that later.

Example #1
Let's say, as an example, that in Step 1 you determined that you want to start a lawn care business.

Now you need to come up with what, exactly, the lawn care business will sell to the customer.

Some ideas could be:
- Grass cutting
- Raking leaves & pine straw

- Trimming bushes
- Watering plants & grass
- Weeding & mulching flowerbeds

Example #2

As another example, let's say that you determined that you want to sell snow cones at fairs and festivals.

Some ideas of what you could sell could be:
- Small snow cone w/ choice of 10 flavors
- Medium snow cone w/ choice of 10 flavors
- Large snow cone w/ choice of 10 flavors
- Bottled Waters

Now, your turn. In your notebook, write down your complete list of products or services that you will sell to your customers.

Congrats! You have completed Step 2. When you are ready go to Step 3.

Step 3: Who Are You Going to Sell To?

So far you have come up with what your business is going to do and what your business is going to sell.

In this step you are going to determine who your business is going to sell to.

This is your customer.

This is a very important step. If you cannot find someone to buy what you are selling you will not have a business.

Who to Aim For
Not everyone is going to be a customer for your business. For example, if you are starting a lawn care business then someone who lives in an apartment will not be a likely customer - because they don't have a lawn!

You need to know what types of people you should be aiming for. These will be the people who are likely to buy what you are selling.

So, in this step you are going to come up with your 'target customer'.

Think of a target. The center of the target is the people that are very likely to buy what you are selling.

The goal, of course, is to aim for the center. You need to reach the people that are very likely to buy what you are selling.

Your Target Customer
In just a few moments you are going to determine who you should be aiming for by describing a typical person who you think would buy what you are selling - your 'target customer'.

Your 'target customer' is one person - real or made up - that would represent the type of customer who would be willing to buy what you are selling.

You could even give this person a name. That way, whenever you are faced with a decision you could think to yourself "Would Sara like this?" or "Would David buy this?".

In your notebook, write down the type of person who would likely buy from you - your target customer.

Below are some questions that can help you describe your target customer.

- What is the age range of your target customer?
- Are they male or female?
- Where do they live?
- Why would they want what you are selling?
- What types of problems would they have that your product/service is solving?
- What is the best way to find them?
- Are there any other characteristics that are unique about your target customer? (For example, they all have a lawn!)

Congrats! You have completed Step 3. When you are ready go to Step 4.

Step 4: Name Your Business

In this step you are going to give your new business a name. Now, your name is important - but not that important.

If someone has never heard of McDonald's before do you think, based on the name, that they would think it is a hamburger restaurant?

Probably not.

So, your name is important but it is not the most important thing.

The most important thing in your business is how many sales you get and how much profit you make. Your name just helps you in the process.

So, in just a few minutes you are going to start brainstorming some names for your business. Here are some tips on naming your business:

Tip #1 - Keep It Simple

You will want people talking about your business. The simpler your name is the easier it is for your target customers to remember.

Tip #2 - Make Sure it is Not Like Another Name

It is vitally important that you do not make your business name like that of another business name. The other business will not like this at all.

For example, you've heard of Dairy Queen, right? They will not like it if you sold ice cream and called your business Dairy King.

Tip #3 - Make Sure a Website Name is Available

Regardless of what type of business you have it is almost always a good idea to have a website. You don't have to start one anytime soon but it would be ideal if you can go ahead and find a website name that is the same (or at least similar) to your business name.

To find a website name you can use a service like Go Daddy (http://godaddy.com) or Google Domains (http://domains.google)

Ok, your turn. In your notebook write down as many ideas that you can come up with for a name for your business.

Once you have written down some business name ideas take the rest of the day to come up with your final name. Ask your friends, ask your trusted adults, ask even your target customers.

Congrats! You have completed Step 4. When you are ready go to Step 5.

Step 5: Let's Make a Profit

The main goal of your business should be to make a profit. Profit is the money that you keep. This is the money that you can use to buy things you want. This is also the money that you can save or re-invest back into your business.

There are just three ways to make a profit:

Way #1: Increase sales
Way #2: Decrease expenses
Way #3: Increase sales <u>and</u> decrease expenses

That's it.

For example, if you had $1,000 in sales for the year and $600 in expenses you would have a profit of $400.

But, let's say that you increased sales to $1,200 and kept expenses the same. Your new profit would be $600!

Let's also say that in addition to being able to increase sales you were also able to decrease your expenses from $600 down to $300. Your new profit would be $900!

As you can see, you can either increase your sales and/or decrease your expenses to increase your profit.

Your Product or Service Profit
To ensure that you will always make a profit each and every time you sell one of your products or services you are about to come up with two things:

The first is the sales price you will charge your customer. The second is all the expenses that will go into providing the product or service to a customer.

To help come up with your sales price and expenses we have created a worksheet that you can fill out for each of your products or services.

At this time go to http://myfirstsmallbusiness.com/worksheets and click on the link called 'Profit Worksheet for a Snow Cone Business'. This is a sample 'profit worksheet' for a Snow Cone business.

While looking at the sample worksheet, follow the steps below to see how we filled the worksheet out for a 'Small Snow Cone' product. Then, you will go through the steps again for each of your own products or services.

Step 1

You will need a worksheet for each product or service you plan to sell. So, in Step 1 on the Profit Worksheet you will write the name of just one product or service. In our example, it is 'Small Snow Cone'.

Step 2

In this column, write down the name of any expenses (e.g. supplies, ingredients, parts) that you must spend to provide just one product or service to the customer.

It is important to only include expenses for just one product or service.

In our Small Snow Cone example here are the expenses to deliver one small snow cone to a customer:

Shaved Ice (6 ounces)
Liquid Flavoring (1.5 ounces)
Paper Cone (1)

If you are going to be selling a service (e.g. a dog walking service) you may not have any expenses - just your time. If that is the case, just left Step 2 blank. However, think through the entire service to ensure you are not leaving out some expenses (like dog poop bags or doggie treats).

Step 3
In this column, write down the cost for each expense to provide just one product or service to the customer.

For example, the liquid flavoring for the snow cones may cost you $10 per gallon. But, to provide just one snow cone to your customer you will only use, say, 1.5 ounces, not a whole gallon. So, you would need to figure out how much it would cost you per snow cone.

Step 4
Add up the expenses and put the total here.

Step 5
Now you are going to come up with a sales price for this product or service and enter it here. This is the price that you will be charging your customer.

The price must be more than your expenses. Ideally a lot more. However, the price should be reasonable. People will not pay $10 for a snow cone, for example. Let's say $2.00.

Now, print and complete a worksheet for every one of your products or services that you offer.

As you start your business you will probably come across expenses that you were not aware of. All you need do is go back to these worksheets and adjust your expenses and your sales price.

Congrats! You have completed Step 5. When you are ready go to Step 6.

Step 6: Your Advertising Plan

On Step 2 you came up with a list of products or services that you are going to sell. In this step you are going to put together an advertising plan for your business.

What is Advertising?
Before your target customers can buy from you they have to find out about you in the first place.

Advertising exists so that your target customers can become aware of your business.

Advertising is all around you. There is advertising on TV, on billboards, on Facebook - it's everywhere.

In just a moment you are going to brainstorm ways to advertise your business.

Remember to Aim
Now, there is one main rule when advertising that you should always remember:

Always aim for your target customer.

That's it. Remember, you are only trying to advertise to your target customer. Not the whole world. Not even your entire city.

You just want to reach your target customer.

It would not make sense for someone starting a lawn care business to advertise in apartment complexes. Why?

Because people that live there don't maintain their grass.

If you are starting a lawn care business you need to aim for your target customer. Your target customers all have one thing in common - they have lawns.

So, in just a few moments you are going start thinking of ways that you can advertise to your target customer.

Below is a list of ideas on how you can advertise. Each target customer is different so not every idea will work for your business. Just use these to help you brainstorm ideas that will work for your target customer.

- Go door-to-door and sell directly to the customer
- Create flyers and hang in popular stores or public areas (e.g. grocery store, laundromat, gym). Remember, always ask for permission!
- Create flyers and give to friends, family, and parents to hand out
- Create a website and promote it to everyone you know
- Advertise on social platforms (e.g. Snapchat, Instagram, Facebook)
- Create a YouTube channel and create videos
- Post an ad on services like Craigslist
- Sell on e-commerce sites like ebay.com or etsy.com
- Set up a referral program for your friends & family (for every customer they send your way you give them a certain amount of the sales as a 'finders fee')
- Call people you know on the phone
- Ask your friends and family who they know that might be interested in your product or service. (Make sure you tell them who referred you.)
- Give away your product or services in exchange for referrals
- Once you get started ask existing customers for referrals

- Write personalized post cards, emails, or letters and send to your target customer
- Create business cards and pass out to your target customers (and even pass out to people who may know others that may be your target customer)
- Ask your parents or other family members to sell for you at their jobs and/or to their friends
- Create signs and post on the side of the road
- Send handwritten thank you notes to your existing customers and ask for referrals

Here are two tips to help you come with some advertising ideas:

Tip #1 - Ask Your Trusted Adult
If you need help coming up with ways to get the word out about your business you can ask an adult you trust.

Tip #2 - See What Your Competitors Are Doing
Another way to come up with some great ideas is to see what your competitors are doing. Don't copy them, however, they are a good source of ideas because they are going after the same target customer you are.

Ok, your turn! In your notebook, write down as many advertising ideas as you can think of.

Take your time. Spend the rest of today brainstorming ideas.

Your Sales Strategy

We already determined that the goal of advertising is to get your target customer to find out about your business and to get them interested.

However, once they are interested you then have to be able to sell the product or service to them.

You can have the best product or service in the world but if you can't sell it then your business will go nowhere.

Selling is critical in business. In fact, it's a business' lifeblood.

Let's say that Eric is starting a snow shoveling business. One of the ways he wants to advertise is to post flyers in local restaurants, laundromats, and grocery stores (with the manager or owner's permission of course).

The flyers could say something like:

"Are you getting buried in snow? I will shovel your driveway for you. Call me for a free quote. You can count on me! Call Eric at 555-1212."

Now, what Eric has done up to this point is advertise. The goal is to get the target customer interested.

What happens when a customer calls? Eric then needs to sell the customer his service.

Here's how to do that…

Selling to Your Customer
We just went over the fact that the goal of advertising is to get a target customer interested in your business. However, it is not enough to just get them interested, you must also get them to take action - to do something.

So, every bit of advertising that you do must entice the customer to take some sort of action.

So, for example, the action that Eric wants his target customers to take on his flyer is to call his number.

You need to tell your target customer what you want them to do. Ideally, only give the customer one action to take. At the most two. Any more than that and the advertising gets confusing.

Here are some examples of actions that you could ask your customer to take:

- *"Call this number"*
- *"Turn right at next light"*
- *"Go to this website"*
- *"Email me"*
- *"Click this link"*

Go back to your advertising list in your notebook and review it. For every advertising idea that you had write down next to it the one or two main actions that you want a customer to take after seeing your advertising.

Again, the reason why we are only asking the customer to take one or two actions is because we don't want to overwhelm the customer. We want them to take a very specific next action.

What Happens Next?

Now let's assume that a customer does take the next action step. In Eric's case a potential customer calls his phone number.

You now must sell your product or service to your customer.

They are obviously interested in your business because they took your action step. Now, it is your job to take an action step.

You step is to sell them - to get them from being an interested customer to an actual customer.

In Eric's case, he will find out a little more about the customer (such as exactly what they need done, their name, and address) and then schedule a time to go to the potential customer's house so he can give them a free quote.

If your business is selling products this step is easier. You would simply let your product do the selling. However, you may want to include in your action step that you would greet the customer or be available for questions or ask if they need any assistance.

In your notebook, write down what exactly you will do once a target customer takes their action step.

Of course, once you start your business your selling strategy will most likely change. But for now, you need to at least have some sort of selling strategy for when a customer takes their action step.

If one of your advertising methods is to directly approach a target customer (for example, go knocking door to door) then continue reading with 'Your Sales Pitch'. If not, then you are complete with this step and you can go to Step 7.

Your Sales Pitch
If one of your advertising methods is to directly approach your customers, either in person or over the phone, it is important to prepare ahead of time what you are going to say to your customers to entice them to buy from you.

In just a few moments you are going to prepare for approaching a target customer by first writing down your sales pitch. It is better to first write down what you want to say to your target customer before you actually say it. That way you can get the wording just right.

Below is a sample script that you can use when approaching your target customers. Read through this script and in a moment you will have the opportunity to write down - in your own words - how you want to pitch to your target customers.

Sample Script

Hello Mr/Mrs. _____(a)_____! My name is _____(b)_____ and I was wondering if you had just a couple of minutes for me to explain how I can help you _____(c)_____. I am actually just starting this business and I would love the honor for you to be one of my first customers.

Would you be open to me _____(d)_____ on a regular basis? The price is only _____(e)_____. Are there any questions I can answer for you?

Below is an explanation of each of the blanks:

(a)   This is your target customer's name. Always refer to them by Mr. or Mrs. (assuming they are an adult). Customers love when you show them respect.

(b)   Your first and last name.

(c)   This is how you are helping the customer (for example, take care of your lawn, shovel your snow, etc.).

(d)   This is a brief summary of a service you are offering them (for example, cutting your grass and trimming your hedges).

(e)   This is the price you identified on Step 5.

Eric's Script

Here is Eric's script so that you can see how he plans to approach a target customer for his snow shoveling business.

Hello Mrs. Smith! My name is Eric Green and I was wondering if you had just a couple of minutes for me to explain how I can help you keep your driveway shoveled during the winter so that you don't have to.

I am actually just starting this business and I would love the honor for you to be one of my first customers.

Would you be open to me shoveling your driveway every week during the winter? The price is only $10 per week. Are there any questions I can answer for you?

Ok, now your turn. In your notebook, write down, in your own words, the script that you want to use to pitch to your target customers.

Good job! As you get further along in your business you will naturally want to adjust your script as you speak to more and more target customers.

Selling Tips

Approaching anyone to buy something from you can seem overwhelming. However, the first few times are the toughest. It gets so much easier the more you do it.

Below are some tips to keep in mind when approaching anyone to buy what you are selling:

Tip #1 - Relax

When you are speaking to a potential customer try to relax. He or she is a person just like you.

The goal of selling is to make both parties happy - them and you. If one party is not happy then don't force it. Just move on to the next person.

Selling is all about finding a win-win for both you and the customer. They win because they get what you are selling. You win because you get their money and, hopefully, their loyalty so they will become a repeat customer and tell their friends.

Tip #2 - Practice
It is important to practice your pitch. Practicing to yourself in the mirror helps. You can also practice to a friend, parent, and/or trusted adult.

Tip #3 - Don't Read
Do not read your script to your customer. This comes across as if you are not prepared. Remember - just relax!

Make sure you have practiced enough to know your sales pitch inside and out.

Tip #4 - Smile
When pitching your customer it is important to smile. Smiling makes you come across as friendly. People want to buy from people who they like. Smiling goes a long way!

Tip #5 - Be Respectful
Especially when selling to adults it is highly important to be respectful. Say things like 'yes ma'am', 'yes sir', 'please', 'thank you', 'Good morning!', 'Good afternoon!'.

Always refer to adults by Mr. or Mrs. and their last name. If you don't know their name 'Ma'am' or 'Sir' works.

Just like with smiling, people love to buy from people they like. If you come across as respectful they will certainly take notice.

Tip #6 - Dress the Part

This goes along with smiling and being respectful. Your appearance and the way you dress need to look professional.

Your customers will judge you on first appearance - before you even open your mouth - so the way you look is very important.

Make sure you are clean, that you smell nice, and that you comb your hair - you get the picture!

Now, you don't have to wear dress clothes - just look nice and professional. It also depends on what you are selling. If you are selling lawn care services you would not need to wear a tie (if you are a guy) - just a nice collared shirt that is tucked in with blue jeans or khakis. For ladies, if you wear a dress or skirt make sure the length is appropriate.

Your customers will likely be adults and so the key is to look nice and professional.

Tip #7 - Expect questions

Selling is a two-way street. You can pitch to your target customers with your script but it is important to ensure that your customers are able to ask questions.

In fact, you should expect that your customers will ask questions so you need to be prepared to answer any questions they have.

To be prepared for questions think of all the potential questions a target customer might ask and go ahead and come up with the answers ahead of time.

You could also ask a trusted adult to help you with these potential questions and answers.

In your notebook, write down the top three questions that you think a customer might have about your product or service and then go ahead and answer them.

Tip #8 - Expect No's

The last tip is that you need to expect people to turn you down. It is okay. Don't get discouraged. Selling is a 'numbers game' in that you must get through a lot of "No's" before you will get a "Yes".

Just because a handful of people said no to you doesn't necessarily mean that your business idea is a bad idea.

Congrats! You have completed Step 6. When you are ready go to Step 7.

Step 7: Get Wise Counsel

Since you have started this plan you have gone through many steps to build your business - and you are almost finished.

But, as with any major project or decision in life it is better to seek the counsel of someone smarter and wiser than you.

This is especially true with a business that you are trying to start.

You have been very focused on planning your business - which is good - but because you have been so focused you may miss some big problems that someone with fresh eyes will be able to easily spot.

So, in this step you are going to find a trusted adult and ask them to review your work thus far. Let's get started.

Think of One Person You Trust

In just a few moments you are going to come up with one person whom you trust and that has a good 'business sense' to be your wise counsel.

This is someone who meets all four of these criteria:

1. You trust them.
2. You care about their opinion.
3. You know they will not just tell you what you want to hear.
4. You think they 'know' about business.

For example, your Grandma may be your #1 fan and will be glad to take a look at your plan. But, as with most Grandmas, they are sweet. She is probably going to tell you that your idea is the best in the world - because she loves you.

That is not what you need. You need someone who can tell you the truth. Even if the truth hurts. It is also ideal if that person has some 'business smarts' about them.

Here are some ideas on who to ask to be your 'wise counsel':
- Your business or economics teacher at school
- Your parents/grandparents/aunts/uncles if they meet the qualifications above
- Your parents' bosses at work
- Your parents' friends who either manage or own a business

- Your friends' parents who either manage or own a business

In your notebook, write down who you want to be your 'wise counsel'. Take some time to think who the right wise counsel should be.

Ask Your Wise Counsel to Help You

You just identified who you want your wise counsel to be. In just a few moments you are going to approach them and ask them to simply do two things:

1. Review your business ideas for each step thus far, and
2. Give you honest feedback.

Ok, at this time go ahead and reach out to your wise counsel and ask them to review your business plan and give you honest feedback.

Make Changes

Hopefully your wise counsel gave you a lot to think about. Not every plan is perfect the first time you write it down - plus, the person that you asked to review your plan has a lot more experience at business than you do - so it is wise to listen to them.

Because of this, you are simply going to take all their feedback and make any adjustments to your plan. So, based on your wise counsel's feedback go back through Steps 1 through 6 and adjust your plan as needed.

Depending on your wise counsel's feedback this could take just a few minutes or it could take several hours.

The idea is that before you actually start your business you have a solid plan in place. Make sure you take the time now to adjust your plan based on your wise counsel's feedback.

Congrats! You have completed Step 7. When you are ready go to Step 8.

Step 8: Get What You Need to Start

In this step you are going to list all of the equipment and supplies that you will need to get started and then you will go ahead and get them.

Now, you just want to list the bare minimum equipment and supplies that are needed just to get started. Once you start making money you will then be able to get better equipment and more supplies.

So, for now, start thinking of the equipment and supplies that you will need to get started.

For example, if you are starting a lawn care business you might list these items that you need just to get started.

- Lawnmower
- Rake
- Gloves
- Lawn Trash Bags
- Gasoline for the lawnmower

Now, it would be nice to have a weed eater, a hedger, and a blower. But, that is not necessary to get started. Again, once you start making some money you can then decide to invest in more equipment and supplies.

In your notebook, write down the bare minimum equipment and supplies that you will need to get started.

Where and How
In just a few moments you will write down where or how you will get the equipment or supplies you just wrote down.

It would be better if you didn't spend any money at all on supplies or equipment. If you ask your parents, grandparents, or other family members I am sure they would be happy to let you borrow equipment.

Now, if you have money saved up (or someone is willing to give or lend you money) you can, of course, purchase the equipment or supplies needed.

However, you should think twice about spending a lot of money (or borrowing money) at this stage. Here's two reasons why:

Reason #1 - Your business idea may change once you get started. You don't want to have spent a lot of money on equipment that you will no longer be able to use.

Reason #2 - If you borrow money from someone you must pay it back - even if your business doesn't make any money. You don't want to have to owe money for equipment or supplies on a business that is not making any money.

So, if your business idea requires that you spend a lot of money or borrow money you may want to re-think your idea and either come up with something new or change your idea so you are not needing to spend or borrow money.

In your notebook, write down how or where you will get the supplies and/or equipment that you listed.

Get What You Need
You have determined what equipment and supplies you need to get started and you have determined how you will get those items. Now, go ahead and start getting all of the items on your list.

Congrats! You have completed Step 8. When you are ready go to Step 9.

Step 9: Prepare to Start

You have spent the last 8 steps preparing to start your business. You have decided what products or services you want to offer and you have gotten all of the supplies and equipment you will need.

In just a few moments you are actually going to create the product or service so that you will be ready to start selling it.

If you are selling a product
If you are selling a product then your goal is to completely build the products and have several of them ready to sell.

For example, if you are selling your homemade jewelry collection you will want to create several of your pieces so that you will have enough to showcase and sell when you start.

If you are selling a service
If you are selling a service then you need to be fully prepared and ready to offer the service.

For example, if you are starting a lawn care service, you will want to ensure that your lawnmower and other equipment is ready and that you have a way to transport your lawnmower and other equipment to your client's house.

It does not have to be perfect
Your product or service does not have to be fully completed. Since you are just starting out it is tempting to spend a lot of time perfecting your product or service. There are two problems with this:

Problem #1 - Your product or service will never be perfect.
You will always continue to improve it.

Problem #2 - Only until you start selling it will you know what improvements you need to make.

The goal is to create what's called a 'Minimally Viable' product or service. This is the minimum required to sell to a customer. Your product or service should be good - but it doesn't have to be perfect right now.

The goal is to start selling. Then you will know, based on customer feedback, what aspects of your product or service you should improve.

Ok, if you are selling a product, go ahead and create your product(s) so that you will be ready to sell them when you start your business.

If you are selling a service, go ahead and prepare the service so that you will be ready when you start your business. (For example, get your lawn mower cleaned and put gas in it.)

Congrats! You have completed Step 9. When you are ready go to Step 10.

Step 10: Start Your Business

You did it! You are at step 10 - the step when you will start your business. I hope you are excited. You have spent the last 9 steps preparing for today. Today you will show the world what you've got.

Before you start your business here are five things to keep in mind:

#1 - Always Keep Updating Your Business Plan
You have a lot of valuable information in your notebook. As you start building your business make sure you keep updating your plan so that you will always have a record of what works.

#2 - Read the Business Tips
Included in the next section are some business tips. These tips contain a lot of helpful information to help you start, build and grow your business.

#3 - Don't Get Discouraged
Starting a business and getting customers is no easy task and one that will probably take a while to get going - so it is important for you to know this and not get discouraged if it seems to be taking a while to get customers.

#4 - Pivot. Pivot. Pivot.

Pivot means to turn. As you start your business you will learn a lot. One of the things that you learn is that your original business idea may need to change - to turn into something else. This is okay and it is natural. If you find that something is not working then you need to pivot - to turn and try something else. Pivoting is good!

#5 - Don't Stop

If you truly believe in your business you need to give it your best shot. So, when it seems like you are not making a lot of progress just try to keep going. Don't stop.

Ok, at this time, go ahead and pick one method of advertising from Step 6 and kick it off and officially launch your business!

On the next few pages are some helpful tips to help you start, build, and grow your business.

Business Building Tips

Tip #1: The Customer Is King

What is a king? It is the top-dog - the guy who calls the shots.

You have a king in your small business - and it's not you - it's your customer.

They are the top-dog. They call the shots.

Why is that? Because the customer is the one who gives you their hard-earned money in exchange for your product or service.

Without the customer your business is dead. Gone.

So, because of this you must not only think of the customer as king - you have to treat the customer as a king.

Everything about your business needs to demonstrate to your customer that you work for them, that you care about their needs, that you want to serve them and that you want to make them happy.

Tip #2: Repeat Customers are Good

Finding new customers is difficult. You first have to advertise and then you have to sell to them. Then, they have to decide if they really want your product or service.

What's better than a new customer? A repeat customer.

This is someone who already bought from you and is coming back to buy from you again.

Repeat customers are good for two reasons:

Reason #1 - You know that your product or service is something that they liked enough to try you again. This proves that people like your product or service.

Reason #2 - You don't have to spend a lot of effort or money getting a new customer to make a new sale.

So, we know that your customer is king. If you truly treat your customer like a king they will be more likely to buy from you again.

Remember, your customer is king. Repeat customers are good.

Tip #3: Referrals are Great

Let me ask you a question - if you saw a commercial for a new restaurant in town would you run out and eat there immediately?

Probably not.

But, what if you went to school and every single one of your friends were talking about this restaurant. They described the food. They described the atmosphere. They loved it.

Would you now want to run out and eat there?

Probably.

Why is that? Because you trust your friends. If they liked something then, because you trust them, you assume you will like it, too.

This is powerful in business. Once you make a sale you should strive to give your new customer such an amazing experience that they will want to tell their friends. Their friends will be more likely to buy from you because they trust their friend - your customer.

This is more powerful than any other advertising that you can do. So, once you have successfully given your customer an amazing experience go ahead and ask them to refer you to their friends.

Remember, your customer is king. Repeat customers are good. Referrals are great.

Tip #4: Ask for Feedback

Now, if your customers are king your goal should be to please them. So, how do you know how to get better at pleasing them?

Ask them.

Once you deliver your product or service to your customer ask them how they liked it and how well you did.

Ask them what they liked best, what they liked least, and what could be improved.

If you ask for honest feedback they will tell you. Once they give you feedback you can then take that feedback and improve your business.

Keep asking for feedback and keep improving your business.

Your customers are king. Listen to the king.

Tip #5: Always Keep Adjusting

You have spent a lot of time building your business. But it is only until you actually start getting customers for your business will you know if your business is working or not.

More likely than not you will find certain parts of your business that are not working that well. At the same you will find things that are working really well.

Here are two rules of thumb:

Rule #1 - Pivot on things that are not working. Remember, pivot is turning things a different direction. If something is not working in your business it is okay to turn a different direction and try something else. If you keep pivoting you will eventually find something that works.

Rule #2 - Do more of the things that are working well. I know this sounds simple but once you find something that is working really well then just do more of it.

For example, if you are trying three different ways to advertise but you are noticing that one way is actually bringing most of your customers then you should put more of your effort in that one way. Do more of it.

All in all, it is perfectly okay to change course once you start your business.

Tip #6: Play By the Rules

Do you know who pays for things like police officers, fire fighters, road repairs, city streetlights, schools, teachers?

We do.

We - as in anyone who makes money - pays for this in the form of taxes.

A tax is simply a fee that you have to pay to the government. The government then takes yours, and everyone else's taxes, and pays for things like the police and fire department, schools, road work, etc.

So, once your business starts making money you will need to pay your share of taxes and other fees that your local government may require.

Now, every single city and state has different tax policies and so it is difficult to give you your next step to ensure that you are paying the right taxes and fees.

So, the best thing to do is to talk to your parents, teachers, or other trusted advisors on what you need to do to be legal in your city and state.

Tip #7: Keep Good Records

There are people in every business who do nothing but keep up with the money and financial 'records' of a business. They are called accountants.

As a small business owner that is just getting started you can do this yourself. However, with accounting things can get really complicated really fast.

But don't worry - here is a very simple and easy way to keep track of your accounting records.

On http://myfirstsmallbusiness.com/worksheets is an "Accounting Records Worksheet" that you can print out. Every single time you either take in money or spend money just record it on this worksheet.

Here's how to fill the Accounting Records Worksheet out.

Step 1: Write the date that you made or spent money in column one.

Step 2: Then, write either "Income" or "Expense" in column two.

Step 3: Write the description of the income or expense in column three.

Step 4: If it is an income just write the total in the Income column (column four).

Step 5: If it is an expense just write the total in the Expense
column (column five).

Step 6: When you fill up a page just total all of your Income and all of your Expenses at the bottom.

Step 7: To find the profit just subtract expense from income.

Below is an example of a few entries…

Date	Is this an Income or Expense?	Description	Income Total	Expense Total
07/01/17	Expense	Gasoline for lawn mower		$20.00
07/06/17	Expense	Lawn trash bags		$16.00
07/09/17	Income	Cut grass for Mrs. Smith	$25.00	
07/17/17	Income	Raked Mr. Barker's front and back yard	$20.00	
Total			$45.00	$36.00
Profit			$9.00	

Tip #8: Be Online and Be Social

One of the best ways to reach new customers is to promote your business online. Many potential customers do their 'research' online before they decide to become a customer.

Think about it - when you and your family want to try a new pizza place in town you probably go to Google or Yelp and find out about it, see what's on the menu, and what the reviews are.

So, this doesn't have to be complicated - in fact since you are starting out it is better if you keep it very simple.

Here are two ways you can promote your business online:

Way #1 - Create a basic website

On this website just have information about you and your business and instructions on how a customer can purchase what you are selling.

Way #2 - Create a 'page' for your business on Facebook

Facebook is a great way for you to interact with potential customers. You can post updates about your business so your friends - and their friends - can see more about your business.

Tip #9: Make A Budget

A budget is a way for you to set goals for your business and then check to see how well you did compared to the goals you set.

Also, the budget is a great way to tell how much profit you can expect. You already know, from Step 5, how much profit you expect to make for every product or service you sell.

On your budget, you can set a goal of how many products or services you think you can sell. Then, you would just multiply the profit by the number that you think can sell to come up with how much profit you can expect for each month.

For example, if you think you can sell 5 products next month and you profit $20 from each sale, then you know you can expect to profit $100 (5 x $20 = $100).

If the following month you can sell 10 products then you know you can expect to profit $200 (10 x $20 = $200).

You can find a "Basic Budget Worksheet" at http://myfirstsmallbusiness.com/worksheets. The budget worksheet is for the one full month after you start your business.

For example, if you are starting your business on March 20th then this budget will be for the entire month of April.

Here are the instructions for completing the budget.

Step 1: Write the month at the top of the budget.

Step 2: In the Step 2 column write down all your products or services

Step 3: In the Step 3 column write down how much profit you will get for each product or service (you determined this while going through Step 5 of the 10-Steps).

Step 4: In the Step 4 column, write down how many products or services you think you can sell for this month for every product or service.

Keep in mind that when you are starting off sales will be slow. You want to be realistic here. It is better to underestimate than overestimate.

Step 5: In the Step 5 column, multiply the profit per product or service (Step 3) by the number you think you can sell (Step 4) to come up with the total profit for the month.

Step 6: At the bottom of the Total Profit column add up the total profit and write that number in the Step 6 box at the bottom.

Step 7: In the Step 7 column, at the very bottom write down any monthly expenses that you will have to pay regardless if you make any sales or not.

Step 8: Now we are going to calculate how much profit you expect to make for the month. To do that just use this formula:

Step 6 - Step 7 = Step 8
(Total Product Profit - Monthly Expenses = Total Monthly Profit)

The number in the Step 8 box is your profit. Do you like your profit number? If so, great! Try to meet that goal.

If you don't like this number and you think it should be higher then adjust either your income or expenses.

Tip #10: Know Your Competitors

It is very important for you to know who you are competing against because you and your competitors will be going after the same people - your target customer.

So, it is important to know your competitors so you can get better than them. You should give your target customer a reason to choose you over your competitors.

Also, by examining your competitors you will come up with some additional ideas on products or services that you haven't already thought of.

So, it is a good idea to do some investigative work by taking a look at all your competitors and just find out a little about them.

By doing this you can determine what makes you unique and what makes you different than all the other businesses going after your target customer.

Competition is Good

You may think that having competitors is a bad thing. You would think that McDonald's would prefer if Burger King didn't exist. Or that Nike would prefer that Adidas didn't exist.

However, here are two reasons why competition is a good thing:

Reason #1
If there is competition it proves that people want what you are selling. If you are the only one on the face of the earth that is selling your product there is probably a reason - and that is that no one wants it.

Reason #2
Competition makes everyone better - and as a result the customers win. Think about it, if McDonald's was the only hamburger restaurant in the United States then they could make the prices as high as they want and could have really bad service.

But, because customers have a choice of hamburger places McDonald's and all of its competitors have to provide top notch service at the best prices - and the customers win!

You are now going to pick 3 competitors and find out a little about them.

Step 1: In your notebook write down your top three competitors.

You may have to do a little research to find your top three competitors. The key is to find the three businesses that are the most like yours that are competing for your target customer.

Most of the information that you will need to answer each of the questions is publicly available. One of the best places to find information on your competitors is to do a simple Google search.

Step 2: For each of your competitors answer the following questions and write them in your notebook:

Question #1: What products or services do they sell?
Question #2: How much do they sell them for?
Question #3: What is one thing they do really well?
Question #4: What is one thing that you think you can do better than them?

As you continue building your business always pay attention to your competition.

The nice thing about your competitors is that they are trying to win over the same target customer as you. So, see what they are doing and see if you can come up with ideas on how to be better.

But remember, always assume that they are doing the same with you!

Tip #11 - Determine Your One #1

Most every business has competition - and this is a good thing.

We talked about the two reasons why this is a good thing in Tip #10:

1. It proves that people want what you are selling.
2. It forces every business to continuously get better.

Now, here's the thing. Because there is competition you have to do one small but critical step. You need to show your target customer why they should buy from you over your competitor.

Think about it, if your target customer has four choices of businesses to pick from and you aren't better than your other competitors then why would your target customer choose you?

They wouldn't.

It is for this reason you need to come up with the one thing that you are going to be the best at - your one #1.

You can't be the best at everything. Neither can your competitors. So, you are going to come up with the one thing that you want to be the best at.

Once you continue building your business this will most likely change. But for now, think about what you want your one thing to be.

Your one thing can be:
- You have the lowest prices
- You offer better customer service
- You are always on time
- You have super friendly service
- You have better tasting products
- You have better looking products
- You have really fast service
- And on...and on...

Ok, so take a few minutes to think and come up with the one thing that you want to be known for. The one thing that you want to be the best at. The one thing that you want to be your #1 reason why a customer would choose you over your competition. Write that down in your notebook.

Congratulations

Congratulations on starting your first business. You have been through a lot and regardless of the 'success' of your business you should be very proud of yourself.

Here's the thing, you have learned so many valuable business concepts that will help you for the rest of your life.

Some adults in their 30's, 40's, and 50's have never even attempted to start a business - but you have.

So, even if your business is not wildly successful (let's hope it is!) you will be able to start another business and get just a little bit better. Then, start a 3rd business and get a little bit better.

In just a few short years, assuming you don't give up, you will be ahead of all your peers and will have so much valuable experience under your belt.

So, the key is to keep going. Don't stop. You have what it takes.

Made in the USA
Columbia, SC
12 August 2020

16118116R00048